THE ONLY WAY OUT

A collection of poetry on healing & recovery

Molly Ziraldo

Copyright © 2019 Molly Ziraldo

All rights reserved.

ISBN: 9781091483590

Inspiration came to me,
like wind through a tree
it rustled my leaves

and I heard a voice say
in the sweet air,

"follow it through if you dare"

The Beginning

THE FLOW

1	The Wonder	Pg 1
2	The Darkness	Pg 15
3	The Healing	Pg 27
4	The Longing	Pg 57

To you,
healing,
keep going.

1
THE WONDER

MOLLY ZIRALDO

A blank page
is an
invitation
for your
soul
to speak

write

THE ONLY WAY OUT

Roam
change direction
break the rules,
draw outside the lines
run wild

Let yourself go,
throw away the map
let your heart be your compass
and run to its' tempo

Find clarity
in what makes it beat faster

And when you get tired
Stop
Rest
And start again.
and again
and again

Just Go

MOLLY ZIRALDO

I travel to places
in which I have no past
in which I have no future

And for once,
I am present

THE ONLY WAY OUT

All music is good
if you like it

All souls will dance
if you let them

MOLLY ZIRALDO

Trust
in the unfolding
of life

For it has
your best interest
at heart

    patience

THE ONLY WAY OUT

It's not about where
you are going

It's about who
you are becoming

surrender

MOLLY ZIRALDO

To live with grace
is to become

softer

as things get
harder

THE ONLY WAY OUT

Your body
is yours

No one can tell you
how to use it

Let it be guided by the wind
and all that soothes it

MOLLY ZIRALDO

Writing
is water
for the soul

drink up

THE ONLY WAY OUT

I want a big life
I want people to see
the truer you are
the more you're set free,

that the strongest amongst us
are still full of fear
and within you lies
the power to heal

MOLLY ZIRALDO

I looked up and thought

*You are so beautiful
what a shame
you can only
be seen
in the dark*

irony

THE ONLY WAY OUT

Quiet, please,
I said to my mind

For it is peace
I'm trying to find

    be still

MOLLY ZIRALDO

Savour yourself.

You will never be
as you are right now

THE ONLY WAY OUT

Create, Dear one

Dig out what's within

Polish it off and
put it on display

They may hate it
They may praise it
They won't get it

You must dig anyway

Start dusting off the gold
which sits upon
the shelves of your heart

This is your art.

MOLLY ZIRALDO

2

THE DARKNESS

MOLLY ZIRALDO

"You've gained weight"
She said.

I couldn't respond
I was too busy picking my heart
up from the floor

"What will do you do?"
She asked.

"Eat salad"
I said.

Good Girl

THE ONLY WAY OUT

The Binge

Every bite
I swear is my last

But hours go by
it all happens so fast

I abandon myself
and turn away

I leave my body
I can't bear to stay

I watch myself
from high above

the girl down below
she is starving for love

For no amount of food
will leave her full

because it's not food
which feeds this soul

Soon it will end
I will come back home,

Full of shame
and all alone.

MOLLY ZIRALDO

You come to me
usually at night
While I'm alone
and out of sight

You leave me
on the bathroom floor,
in my own world
locked up behind a door

Tears in my eyes
I know you tried your best
But every time you try
we end up in this mess

My friend, Bulimia

THE ONLY WAY OUT

I wish I could call
my body home
But all I know
is a desire to roam

Anger provides
my body with heat
So I kick myself out
back on to the streets

homesick

MOLLY ZIRALDO

In all my lows, moments of desperation, nights on the bathroom floor bent over in exhaustion, on my knees praying for it to end. I always wanted a sign.

I always wanted God to talk to me.

He never did

THE ONLY WAY OUT

Down in the bottom it hurts like hell
You're all alone
You have no one to tell

You mop up your anger,
with your own heart
and convince yourself tomorrow
will be a new
start

MOLLY ZIRALDO

The emotional residue
of a binge,
is the hardest
to wash off

There is no shower for the soul

THE ONLY WAY OUT

I thought I had it,
thought I was in the clear

But oh sweet girl,
you thought wrong my Dear

You fell back down,
and slipped through a crack

You landed square,
right on your back

Get up

MOLLY ZIRALDO

The pages keep turning,
but the story
stays the same

plot twist please

THE ONLY WAY OUT

The Break Up

You found me when I had no one to tell
You found me when I had already fell

You picked me up and showed me how
To you each week, I began to bow

You left me hurt and out of shape
But I kept you on, like a protective cape
I tried so hard to take you off,
But I was too broken, too bruised and soft

You crushed my soul
and you crushed my spirit
Joy was a feeling, I could no longer feel it

But we were friends,
just us two
You held all the secrets
no one else knew

But I need to heal now
You need to go away

I need to move on,
is what I'm trying to say

MOLLY ZIRALDO

3

THE HEALING

MOLLY ZIRALDO

It all poured out one night
after so many years
of pouring
in

THE ONLY WAY OUT

In me
are words
in the womb of my throat
waiting
to be birthed

speak up

MOLLY ZIRALDO

Be ready.

For when you start your journey
with an intent to heal,
You'll go through shit

It's part of the deal

THE ONLY WAY OUT

I'm afraid
I'll never get better

I'm afraid
I'll never know
who I'm meant to be

motivation

MOLLY ZIRALDO

Recovery is a labyrinth
Round and around
up and down,
lost and found
dizzy
frustrated
angry
exhausted

Downward spirals and beautiful risings
The sense of knowing where you are and why
Thinking you've got it,
but then, you lose it

Momentum forward,
running faster, feeling better
Only to realize,
another block, another slip

Where am I?
How did I get here?

Remember what you've learned
Remember how far you've come

Turn around
Start again
Try, again

Because,
the only way out
is through

THE ONLY WAY OUT

Become a student
of your recovery

stay curious

MOLLY ZIRALDO

Dear Body,

I'm sorry.

I'm sorry for all I've said, for all I've done
and for all I didn't do

I'm sorry for my thoughts, my actions
and how I lied to you

I'm sorry for the guilt, the shame
and what I've put you through

I'm sorry for the blame, the pain,
I really, never meant to

   forgive me

THE ONLY WAY OUT

Today is hard
Today I don't see a way out
Today I want to run
Today I want to give up
Today I don't see things ever changing
Today I feel like a failure
Today I can't stand to be in this body
Today I can't bear to look at this face
Today recovery feels overwhelming
Today healing seems impossible
Today I feel like I can't
Today my dreams seem so far away
Today will soon be over

Tomorrow will be different.

MOLLY ZIRALDO

2 steps forward
1 step back

The belief in myself
left barely in tact

the relapse

THE ONLY WAY OUT

Love it free

To let something go
you must love it first

Love it for the good it gave you,
love it for the pain it placed within your heart

Love is the tonic which loosens your grip
and lets it slip away

MOLLY ZIRALDO

Moving stills my mind
so that my thoughts can be kind

Moving soothes my soul
and lets my heart feel full

In movement we find grace
the courage to look
ourselves in the face

We were given these bodies
to express as we please
so I hope you come to your mat
with ease.

THE ONLY WAY OUT

Softness
can be
the toughest
thing
of all

breath

MOLLY ZIRALDO

I am calling my body
back home
to me

yoga

THE ONLY WAY OUT

Like I need to stretch my body
so that the energy can move

I need to tell my story
so that my heart can be soothed

MOLLY ZIRALDO

When you peel
back the layers,
it might make you cry

THE ONLY WAY OUT

There is a lot
about to blossom

And I don't know
what will grow

But I know,
it will be beautiful

MOLLY ZIRALDO

Create

It's time to sleep
Let the thoughts go
For there is nothing new
they have left to show

Awake in the morning
and start again
Thankful you're free
to put paper to pen

THE ONLY WAY OUT

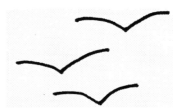

Knowing what feeds me
has freed me

MOLLY ZIRALDO

My words,
spill out
and onto the page

Like luring animals
out from their cage

set them free

THE ONLY WAY OUT

I want you to know you can overcome the pain which has bruised your heart.

I want you to know you are deserving of love and all your heart yearns for.

I want you to know you don't need to hide because we all need connection. Intimacy will keep you alive.

I want you to know you are beautiful. That your beauty is not found in your size or your shape or the features of your face that you so wish to change.

I want you to know you'll get through it. You will always get through it.

MOLLY ZIRALDO

Take care of this container of yours
it carries the essence of your being

For a cracked vase,
cannot be home
to blossoming flowers

THE ONLY WAY OUT

I need to gather
the parts of me
scattered across the floor

For last night
I dropped them
heart, mind, body and soul

They fell through my hands
And I'm on my knees this morning
picking up the pieces

Putting myself
back together
again.

MOLLY ZIRALDO

Healing

Do not rush the process

Each moment
holds within it
its' own purpose

THE ONLY WAY OUT

I ate your words,
they hit the spot.

And finally
I was full.

MOLLY ZIRALDO

And sometimes
we fall,
one more time

Because there was
something
down there
we had left to find

a lesson

THE ONLY WAY OUT

Love lives
within the attention
we give
our needs

MOLLY ZIRALDO

Give yourself
the gift of
presence

and a new ending
will write
itself

THE ONLY WAY OUT

Healing happens,
drip by drip

And finally,
one day
the bucket
is full

MOLLY ZIRALDO

4

THE LONGING

MOLLY ZIRALDO

We all have that song
that reminds us of
someone

A melody that unleashes
all things left
undone

turn it up

THE ONLY WAY OUT

Show me your roots
and
I'll show you mine

vulnerability

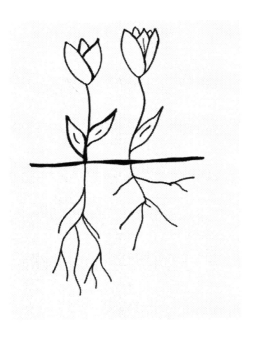

MOLLY ZIRALDO

You never said
I love you
But
I know you do

Dad

THE ONLY WAY OUT

It doesn't need to go
It doesn't need to grow
Just let it be

MOLLY ZIRALDO

I want you to take my hand
I will listen to what you say
I want to close my eyes,
because you already know the way

I want to fall into your presence,
let your words melt my bones
I want your eyes to see my soul
and for you to feel like home

THE ONLY WAY OUT

Don't be afraid to hurt me.

For nobody has broken my heart
more times than myself

MOLLY ZIRALDO

Words in me
like a melting pot

I can stir them around
yet have no courage
to serve them up

I wish you knew

THE ONLY WAY OUT

The truth is, I want to know you. I want to know what you eat for breakfast, how you cook your eggs or if you even do. I want to know how long you take in the shower and the smell of your closet. I want to know what makes you mad and what makes you feel joy and how you express them both. I want to know the sound of your voice when you're tired. I want to feel your hand wrapped around my waist and the heat of your breath upon the back of my neck.

MOLLY ZIRALDO

I don't even know
if I really want in

I just want to know
I was invited

THE ONLY WAY OUT

"I'm in love with my ex"
A left hook to the face, but I wore no gloves
just a smile on my face

When I said the weight had lifted
it wasn't a lie, a part of me had shifted
I was hollower inside

For this was not a break-up, because we never were
I wondered what would happen
with you, I wasn't sure

We'd come so close, yet remained so far
All truth kept inside me
locked up within a jar

And soon, over time, our flame lost light
I thought of you often, but never put up a fight

I never gave you a reason to stay,
weeks turned to months,

You floated away

MOLLY ZIRALDO

Your words
take the wind
out of me

In all the wrong ways

THE ONLY WAY OUT

He said he didn't want me
and when he finally did,
I was drained of all
the love
I once had

    timing

MOLLY ZIRALDO

The day you got married
you texted me

I wonder if she knew?

She did

THE ONLY WAY OUT

Do we control the outcome
or is the book already written?
We can try with all our might to push
when all we must do is listen

Listen to the voice
that speaks from within
It will tell you when to stop
and when you should begin
This is the voice which always knows best
like when we should leave
and when we should rest

Yet I want to know the answers
and how this will end
For I hate the doubt and worry
that uncertainty can lend

It's hard to keep calm
when so much is at stake,
I want to know now
if this choice is a mistake

But if it is already written
for I can relax
Keep peace of mind
and my hope in tact

And if I wander off course
fate will turn me around,
Because life always lead us
lost and then
found

MOLLY ZIRALDO

And I think about the day
we cross paths on the street

The universe conspiring
allowing us to meet

I wonder what would happen
I wonder what we'd say

I wonder what we'd think
as we both walked away

What if?

75

MOLLY ZIRALDO

THE AUTHOR

Molly Ziraldo is from St. Catharines, Ontario, Canada. She grew up as a competitive figure skater and gymnast, and later skated professionally with Disney on Ice. She struggled with bulimia and depression, in silence, for nearly 20 years and hopes that in sharing her story, others will find courage to do the same and know they're not alone.

Instagram @mziraldo

Manufactured by Amazon.ca
Bolton, ON